W9-BCG-517

GRAPHIC BIOGRAPHIES

GEORGE WASHINGTON CARVER
Ingenious Inventor

by Nathan Olson

illustrated by Keith Tucker

Consultant:
Tanya Zanish-Belcher, Associate Professor
Special Collections and University Archives
Iowa State University
Ames, Iowa

Capstone press

Mankato, Minnesota

Graphic Library is published by Capstone Press,
151 Good Counsel Drive, P.O. Box 669, Mankato, Minnesota 56002.
www.capstonepress.com

Printed in the United States of America

1 2 3 4 5 6 11 10 09 08 07 06

Library of Congress Cataloging-in-Publication Data
Olson, Nathan.
George Washington Carver: ingenious inventor / by Nathan Olson; illustrated by Keith Tucker.
p. cm.—(Graphic library. Graphic biographies)
Includes bibliographical references and index.
ISBN-13: 978-0-7368-5484-9 (hardcover)
ISBN-10: 0-7368-5484-3 (hardcover)
1. Carver, George Washington, 1864?–1943—Juvenile literature. 2. African American agriculturists—Biography—Juvenile literature. 3. Agriculturists—United States—Juvenile literature. I. Title. II. Series. III. Keith Tucker, illus.
S417.C3O47 2006
630.92—dc22 2005031248

Summary: In graphic novel format, tells the life story of plant scientist and inventor George Washington Carver.

Art Director
Bob Lentz

Storyboard and Production Artist
Alison Thiele

Production Designer
Renée T. Doyle

Editor
Erika L. Shores

Editor's note: Direct quotations from primary sources are indicated by a yellow background.

Direct quotations appear on the following pages:

Page 10 (both), from Rackham Holt's interview with George Washington Carver as quoted in *George Washington Carver, An American Biography* by Rackham Holt, (Garden City, New York: Doubleday, 1963).

Page 16, from *The Story of My Life and Work* by Booker T. Washington, (Toronto: J. L. Nichols, 1900).

Page 24, from a letter by George Washington Carver to Jimmie Hardwick as quoted in *George Washington Carver In His Own Words* edited by Gary R. Kremer, (Columbia, Missouri: University of Missouri Press, 1987).

Capstone Press thanks Lana Henry, chief ranger, George Washington Carver National Monument, Diamond, Missouri, for reviewing this book.

TABLE OF CONTENTS

Chapter 1

SLAVE TO ORPHAN

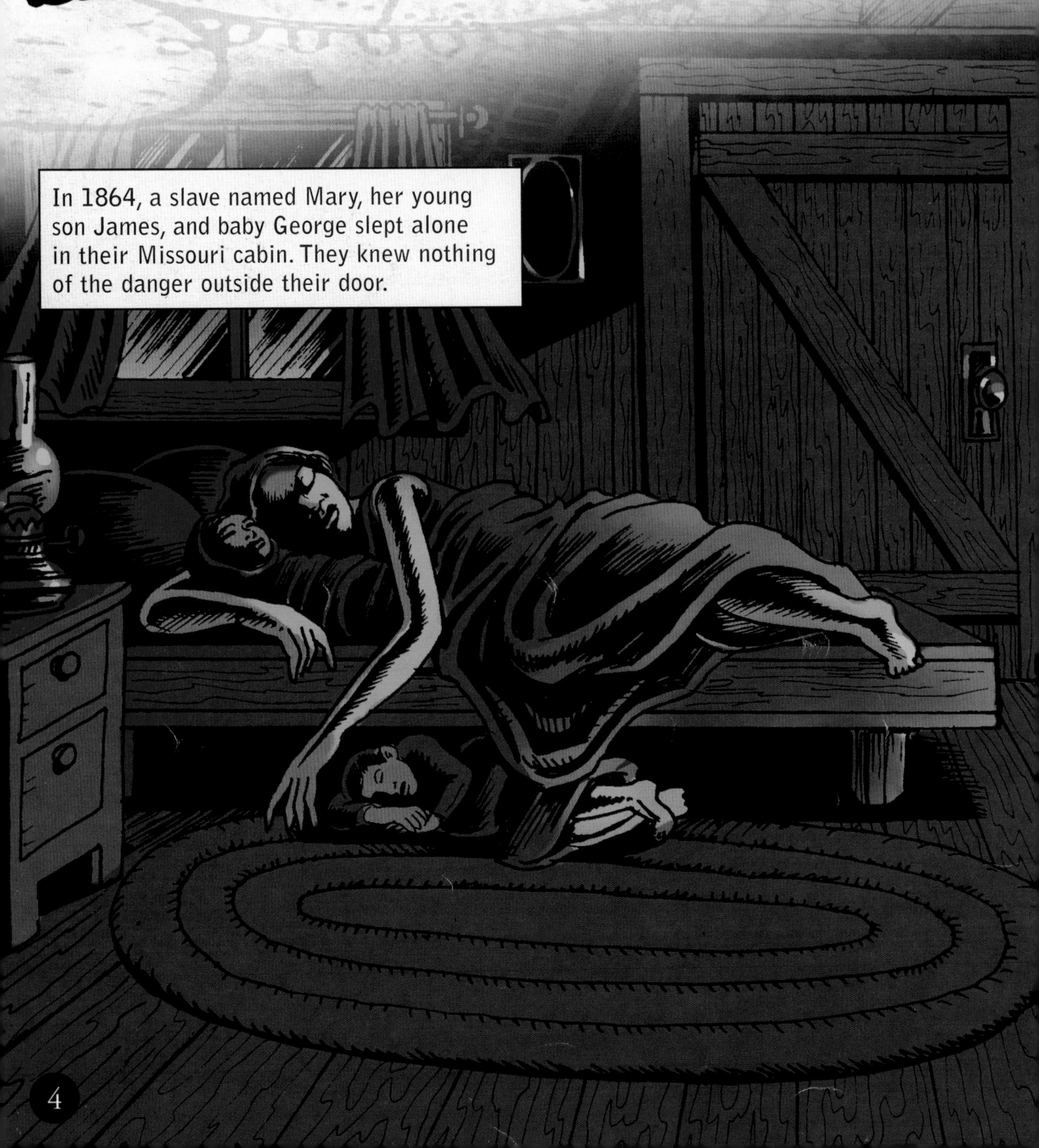
In 1864, a slave named Mary, her young son James, and baby George slept alone in their Missouri cabin. They knew nothing of the danger outside their door.

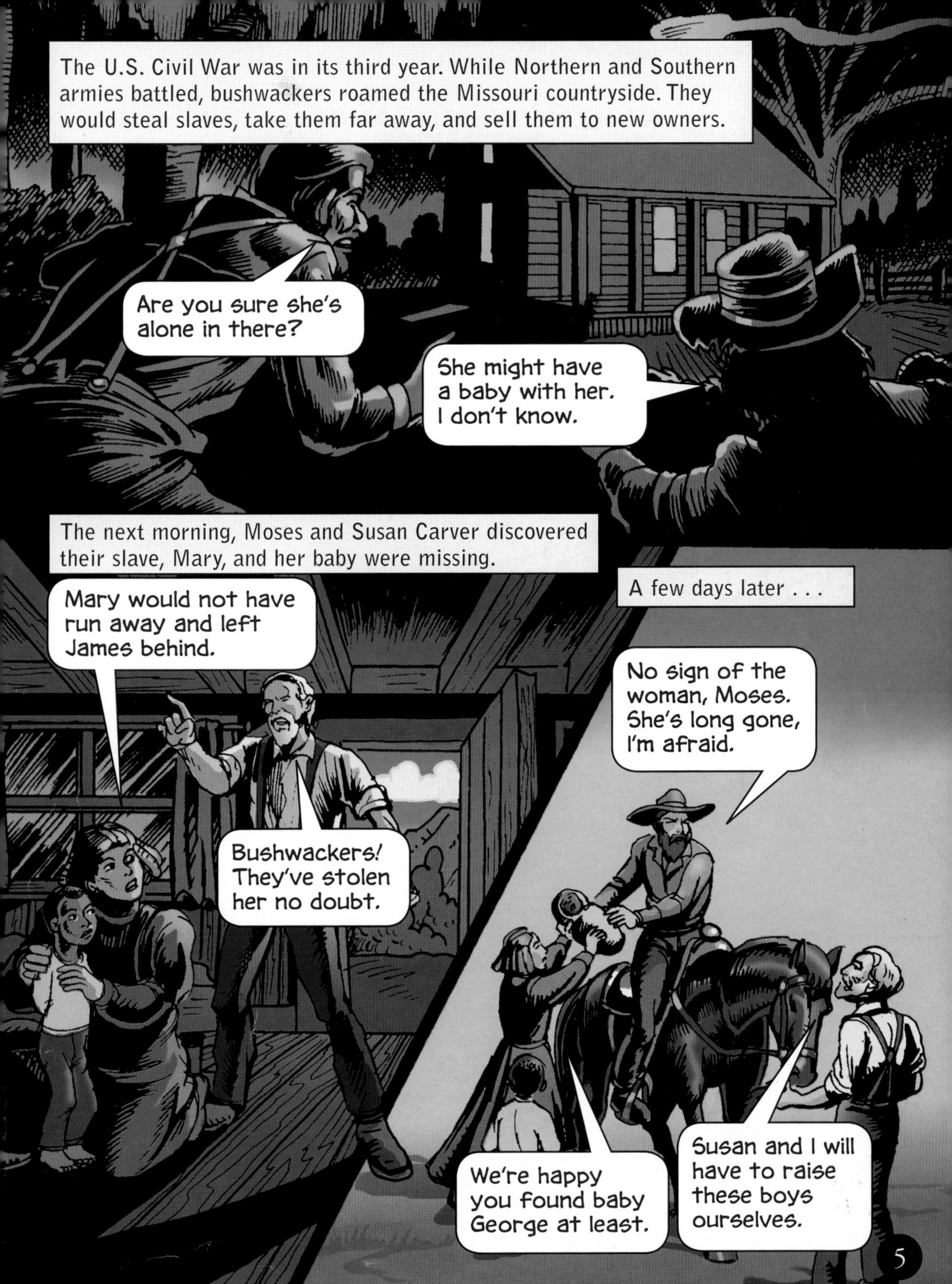
The U.S. Civil War was in its third year. While Northern and Southern armies battled, bushwackers roamed the Missouri countryside. They would steal slaves, take them far away, and sell them to new owners.
Are you sure she's alone in there?
She might have a baby with her. I don't know.
The next morning, Moses and Susan Carver discovered their slave, Mary, and her baby were missing.
Mary would not have run away and left James behind.
Bushwackers! They've stolen her no doubt.
A few days later . . .
No sign of the woman, Moses. She's long gone, I'm afraid.
We're happy you found baby George at least.
Susan and I will have to raise these boys ourselves.

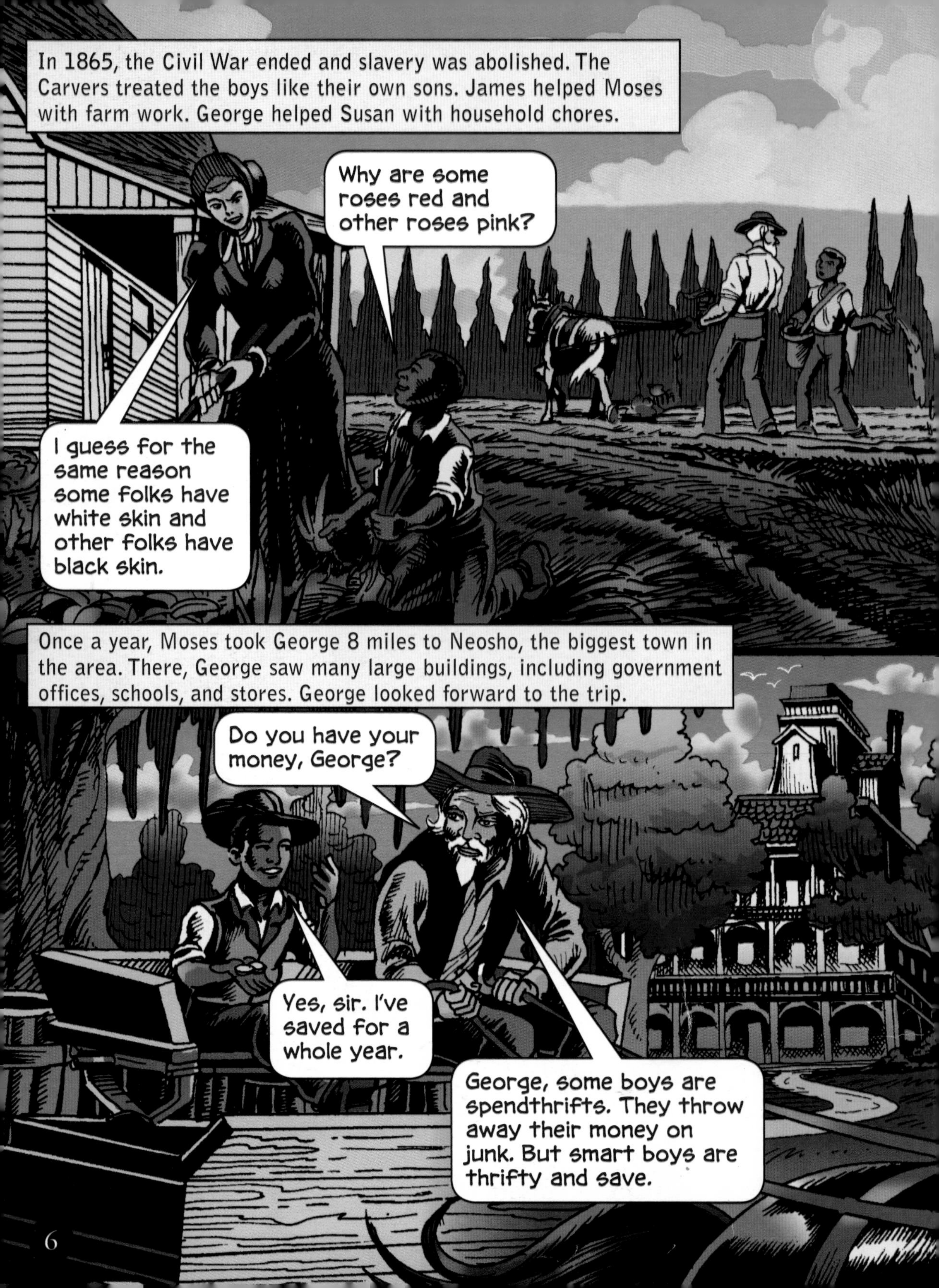
In 1865, the Civil War ended and slavery was abolished. The Carvers treated the boys like their own sons. James helped Moses with farm work. George helped Susan with household chores.
Why are some roses red and other roses pink?
I guess for the same reason some folks have white skin and other folks have black skin.
Once a year, Moses took George 8 miles to Neosho, the biggest town in the area. There, George saw many large buildings, including government offices, schools, and stores. George looked forward to the trip.
Do you have your money, George?
Yes, sir. I've saved for a whole year.
George, some boys are spendthrifts. They throw away their money on junk. But smart boys are thrifty and save.

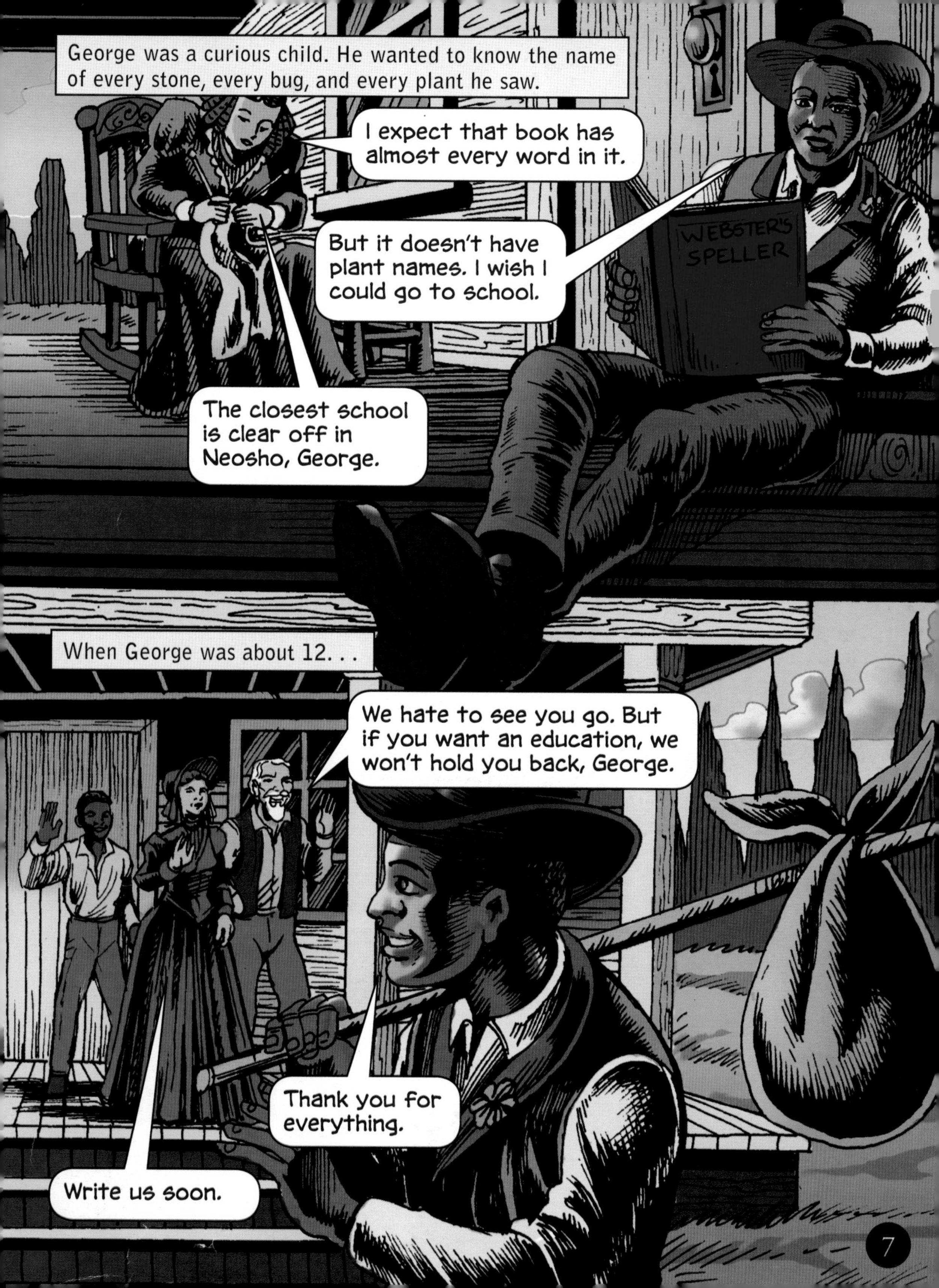

George was a curious child. He wanted to know the name of every stone, every bug, and every plant he saw.
I expect that book has almost every word in it.
WEBSTER'S SPELLER
But it doesn't have plant names. I wish I could go to school.
The closest school is clear off in Neosho, George.
When George was about 12. . .
We hate to see you go. But if you want an education, we won't hold you back, George.
Thank you for everything.
Write us soon.

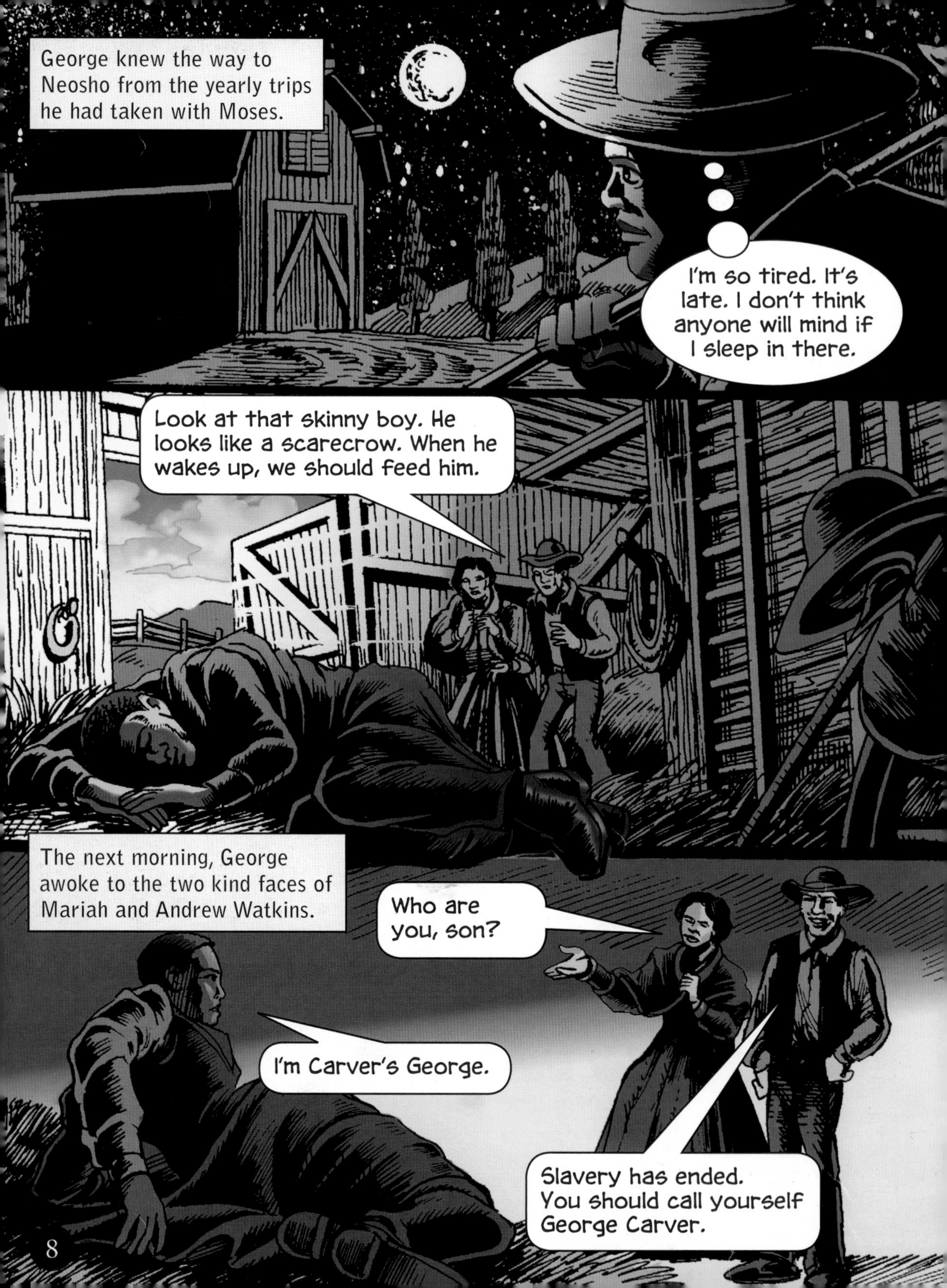
George knew the way to Neosho from the yearly trips he had taken with Moses.
I'm so tired. It's late. I don't think anyone will mind if I sleep in there.
Look at that skinny boy. He looks like a scarecrow. When he wakes up, we should feed him.
The next morning, George awoke to the two kind faces of Mariah and Andrew Watkins.
Who are you, son?
I'm Carver's George.
Slavery has ended. You should call yourself George Carver.

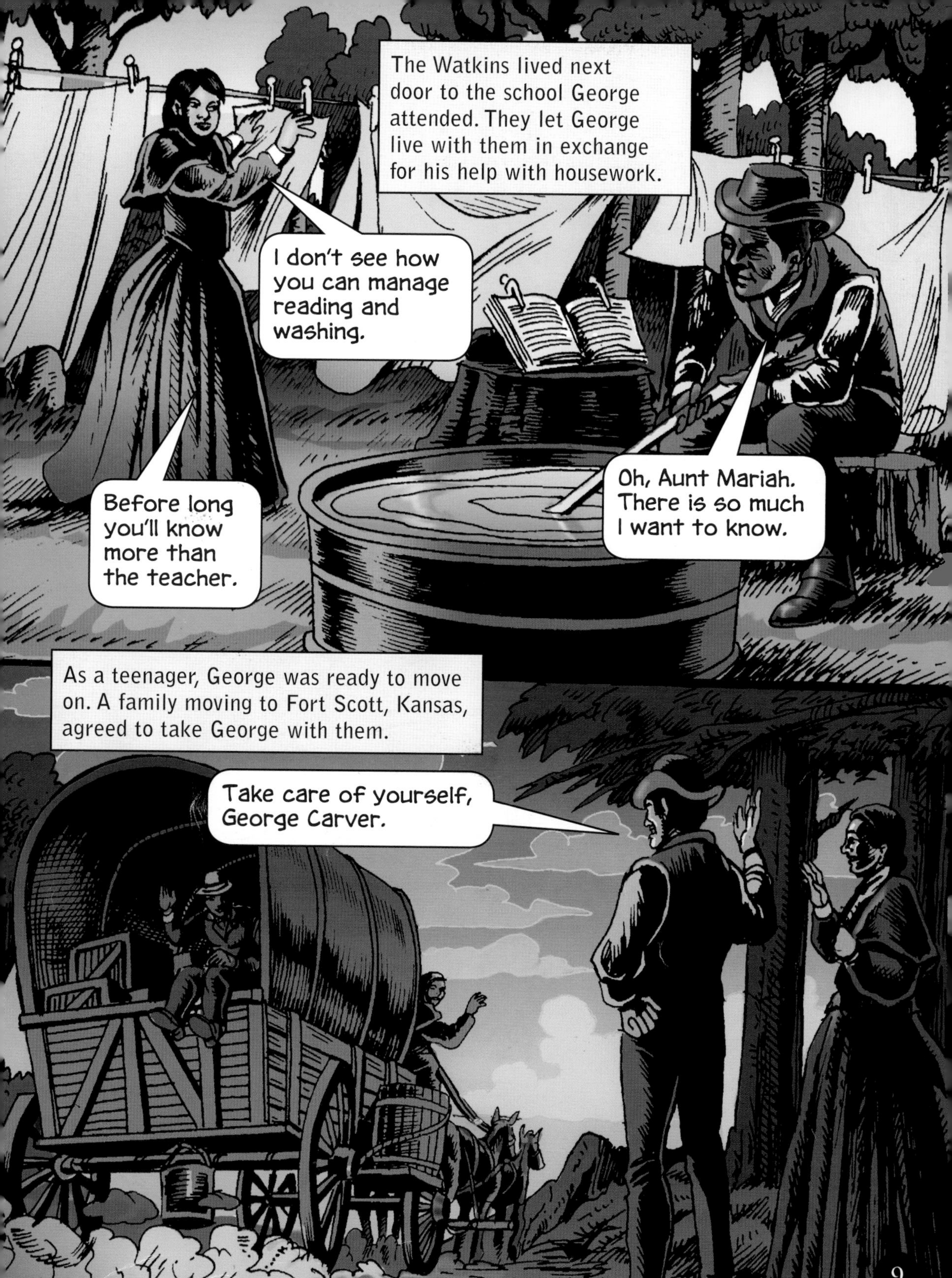
The Watkins lived next door to the school George attended. They let George live with them in exchange for his help with housework.
I don't see how you can manage reading and washing.
Oh, Aunt Mariah. There is so much I want to know.
Before long you'll know more than the teacher.
As a teenager, George was ready to move on. A family moving to Fort Scott, Kansas, agreed to take George with them.
Take care of yourself, George Carver.

Chapter 2
ON HIS OWN

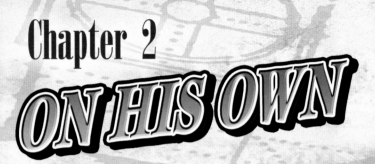

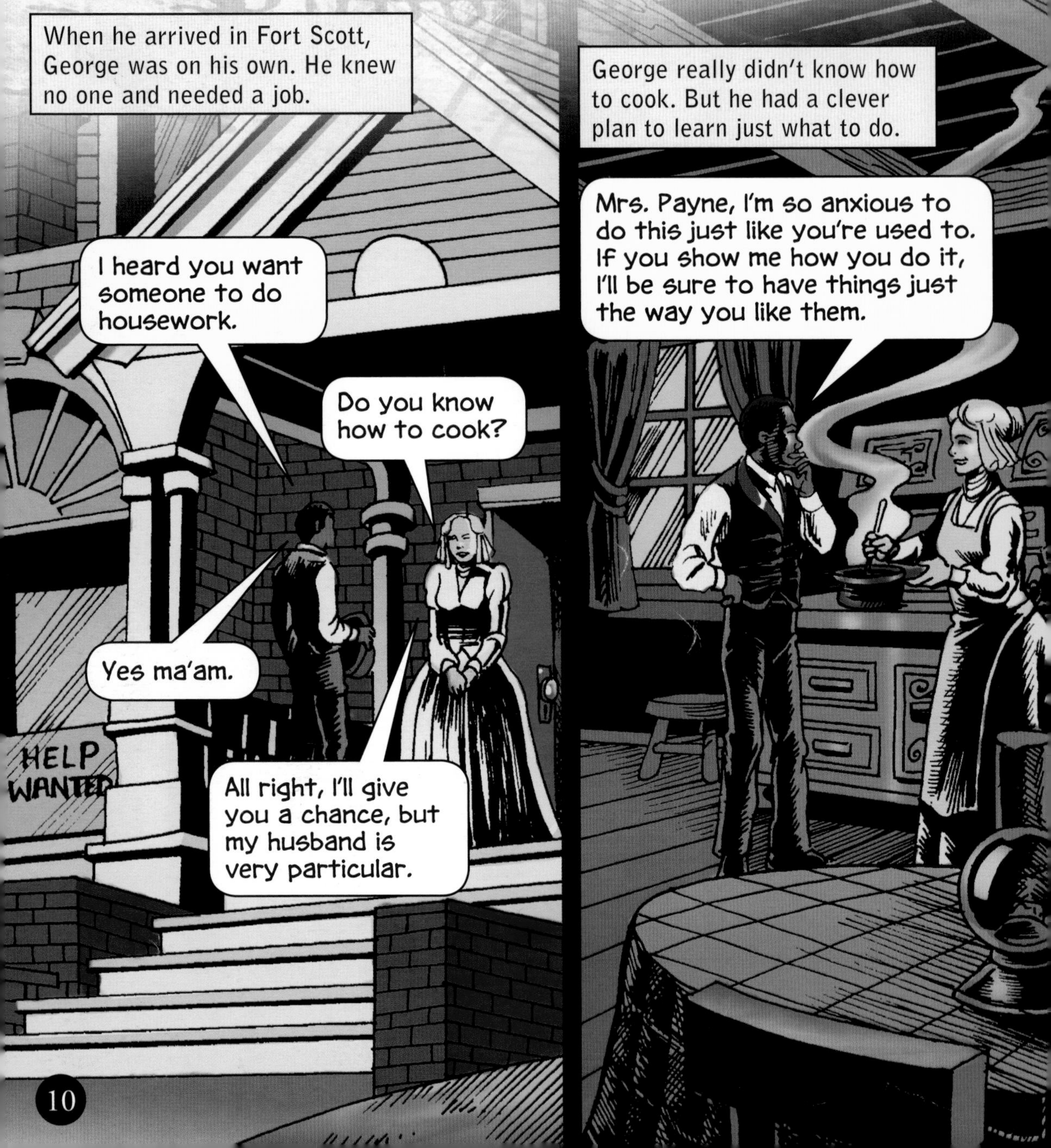
When he arrived in Fort Scott, George was on his own. He knew no one and needed a job.
I heard you want someone to do housework.
Do you know how to cook?
Yes ma'am.
HELP WANTED
All right, I'll give you a chance, but my husband is very particular.
George really didn't know how to cook. But he had a clever plan to learn just what to do.
Mrs. Payne, I'm so anxious to do this just like you're used to. If you show me how you do it, I'll be sure to have things just the way you like them.

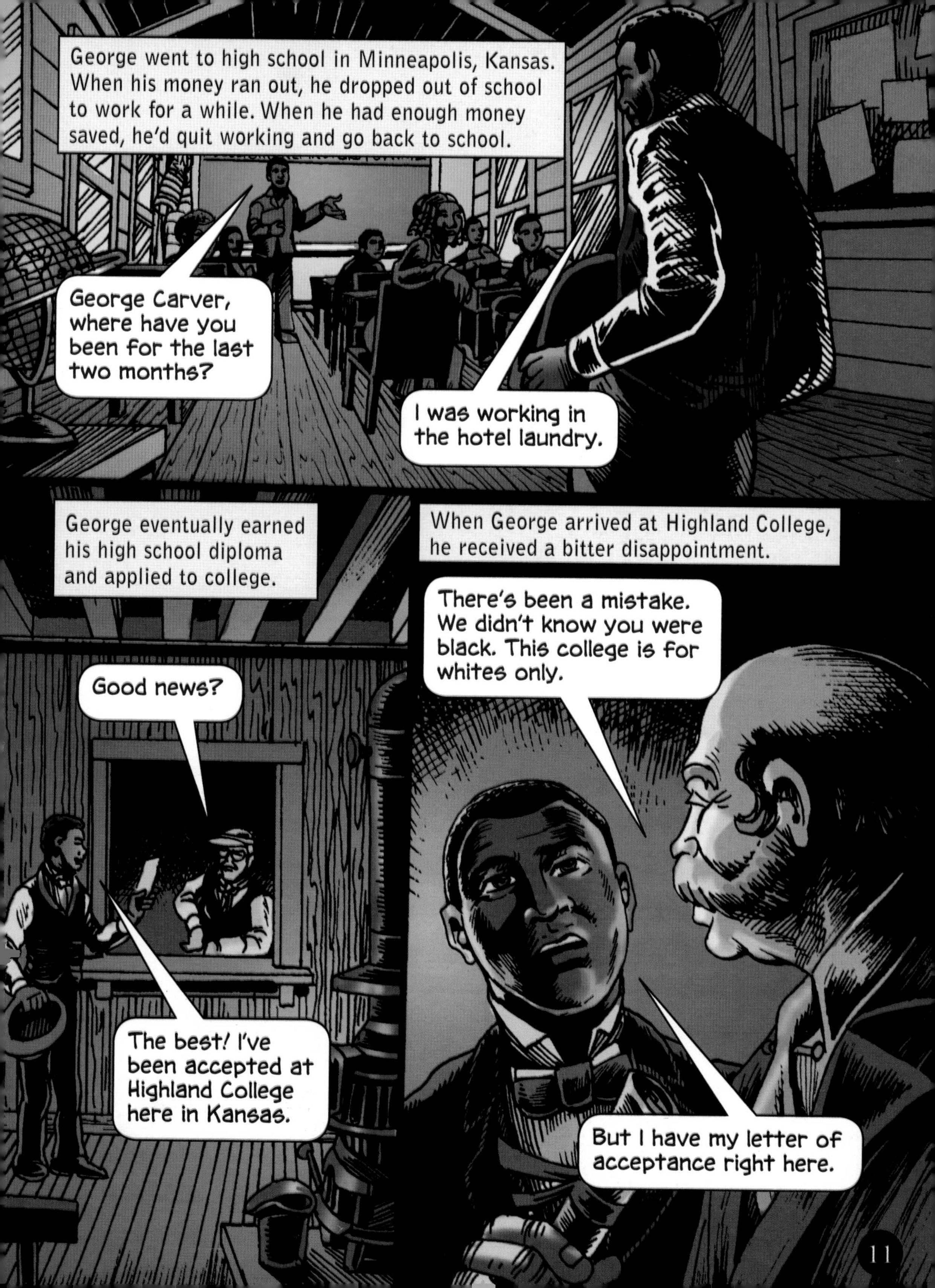
George went to high school in Minneapolis, Kansas. When his money ran out, he dropped out of school to work for a while. When he had enough money saved, he'd quit working and go back to school.
George Carver, where have you been for the last two months?
I was working in the hotel laundry.
George eventually earned his high school diploma and applied to college.
Good news?
The best! I've been accepted at Highland College here in Kansas.
When George arrived at Highland College, he received a bitter disappointment.
There's been a mistake. We didn't know you were black. This college is for whites only.
But I have my letter of acceptance right here.

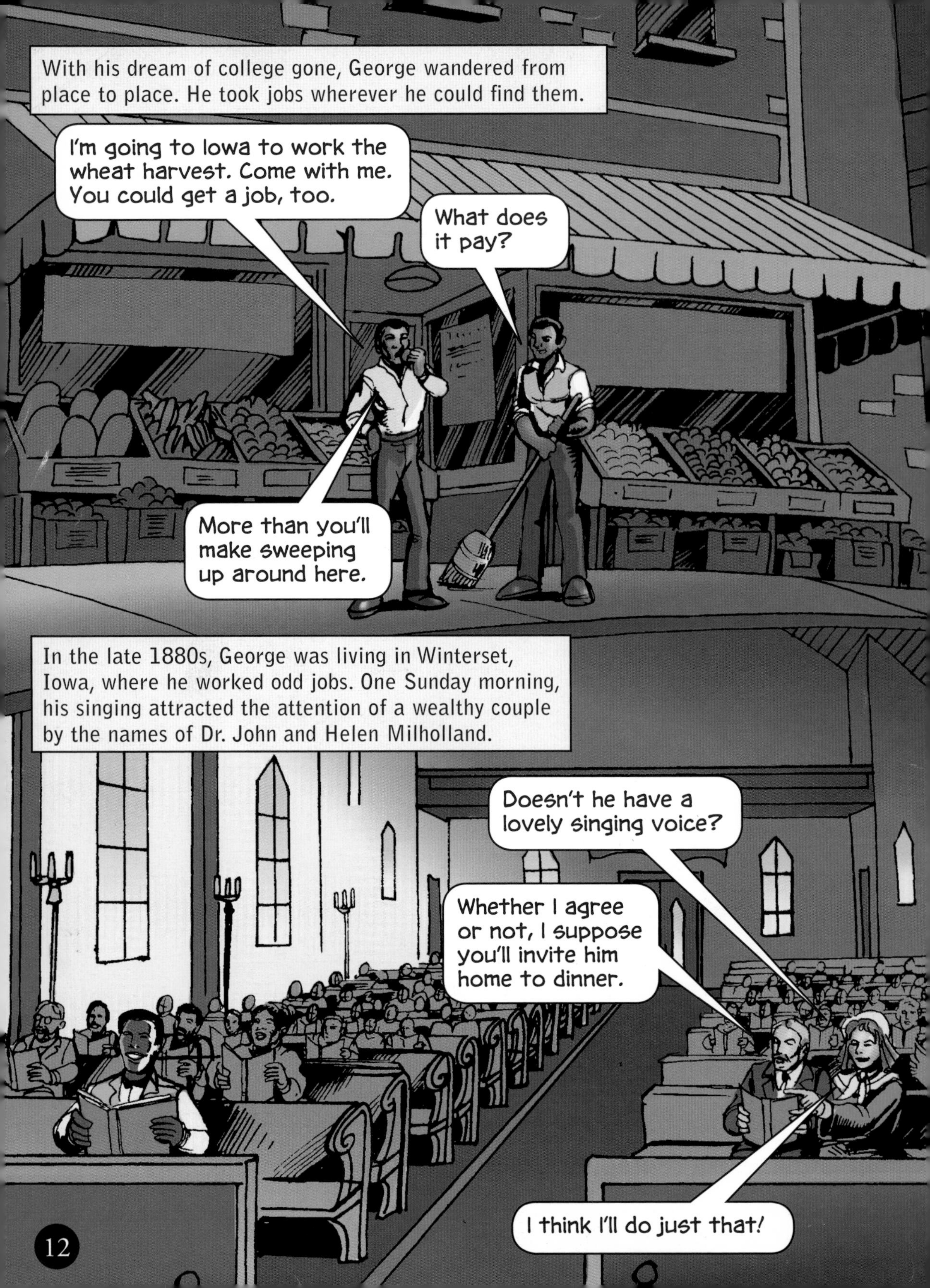
With his dream of college gone, George wandered from place to place. He took jobs wherever he could find them.
I'm going to Iowa to work the wheat harvest. Come with me. You could get a job, too.
What does it pay?
More than you'll make sweeping up around here.
In the late 1880s, George was living in Winterset, Iowa, where he worked odd jobs. One Sunday morning, his singing attracted the attention of a wealthy couple by the names of Dr. John and Helen Milholland.
Doesn't he have a lovely singing voice?
Whether I agree or not, I suppose you'll invite him home to dinner.
I think I'll do just that!

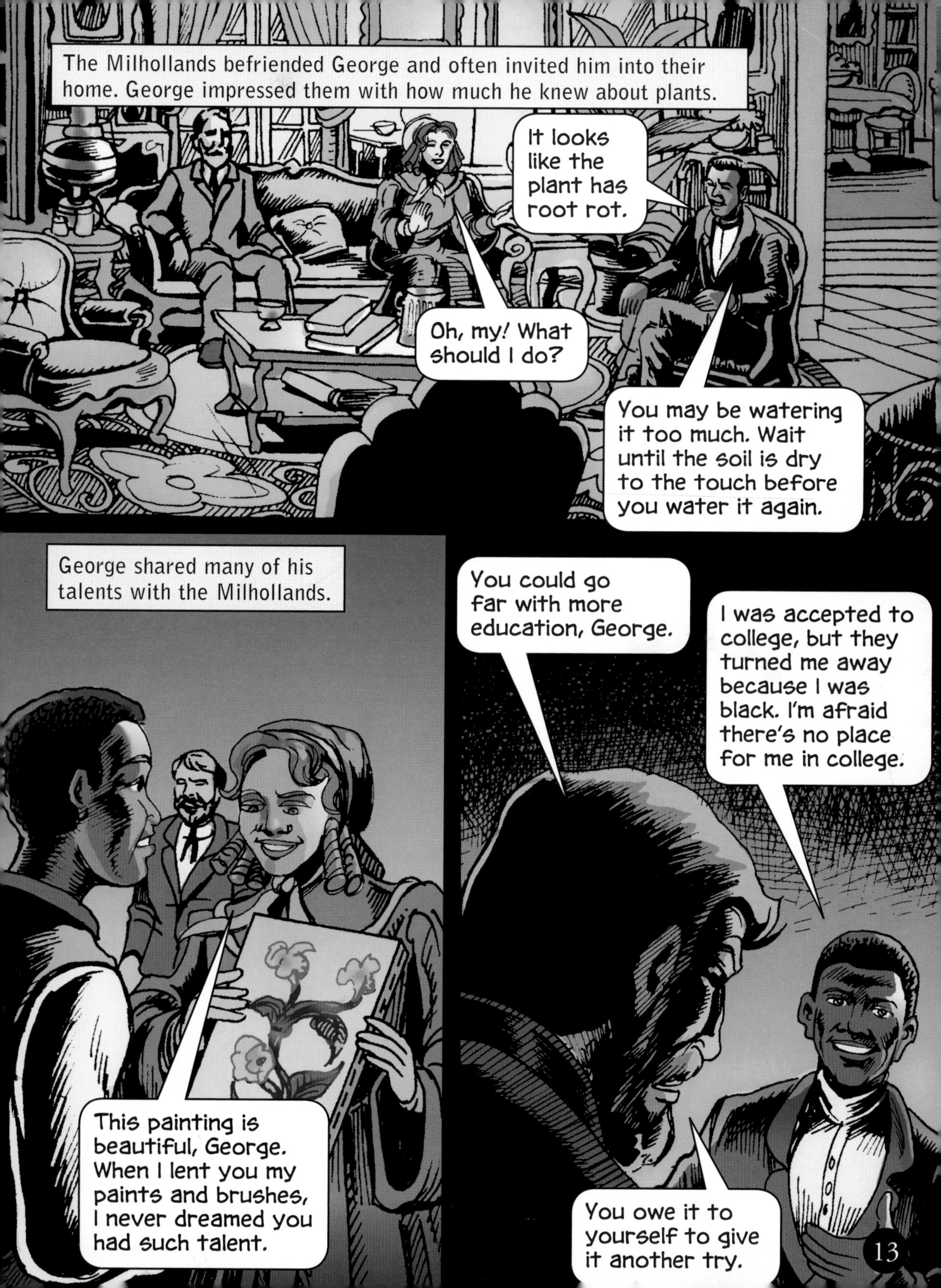

The Milhollands befriended George and often invited him into their home. George impressed them with how much he knew about plants.
It looks like the plant has root rot.
Oh, my! What should I do?
You may be watering it too much. Wait until the soil is dry to the touch before you water it again.
George shared many of his talents with the Milhollands.
This painting is beautiful, George. When I lent you my paints and brushes, I never dreamed you had such talent.
You could go far with more education, George.
I was accepted to college, but they turned me away because I was black. I'm afraid there's no place for me in college.
You owe it to yourself to give it another try.

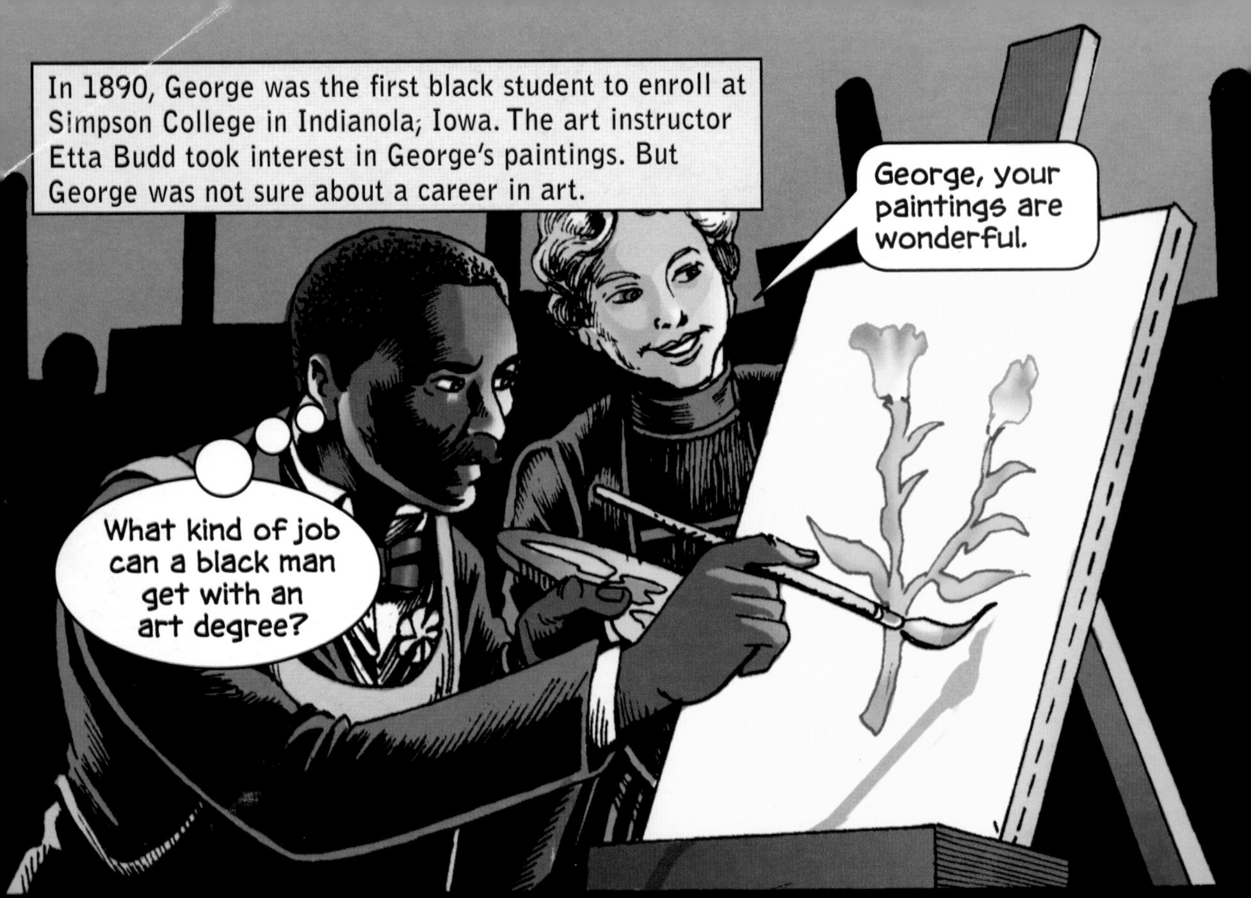
In 1890, George was the first black student to enroll at Simpson College in Indianola, Iowa. The art instructor Etta Budd took interest in George's paintings. But George was not sure about a career in art.
George, your paintings are wonderful.
What kind of job can a black man get with an art degree?

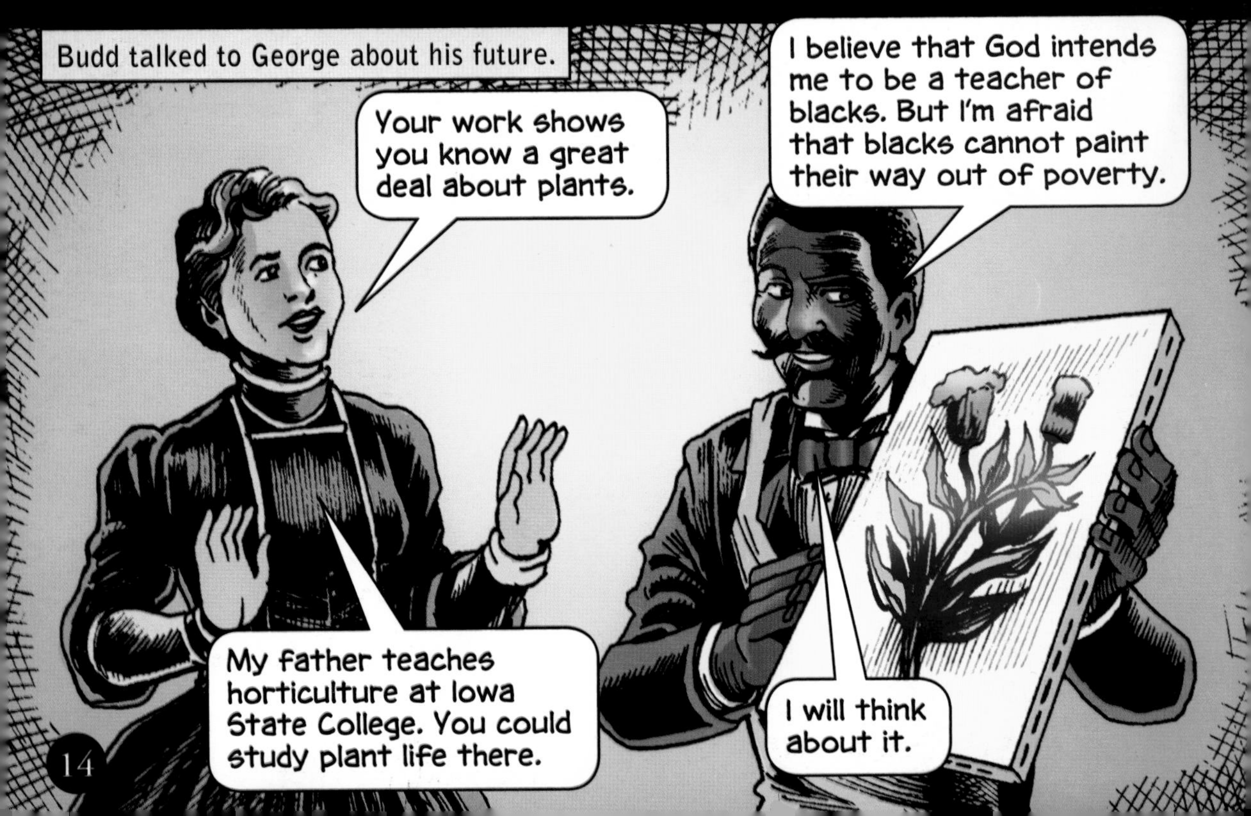
Budd talked to George about his future.
Your work shows you know a great deal about plants.
I believe that God intends me to be a teacher of blacks. But I'm afraid that blacks cannot paint their way out of poverty.
My father teaches horticulture at Iowa State College. You could study plant life there.
I will think about it.

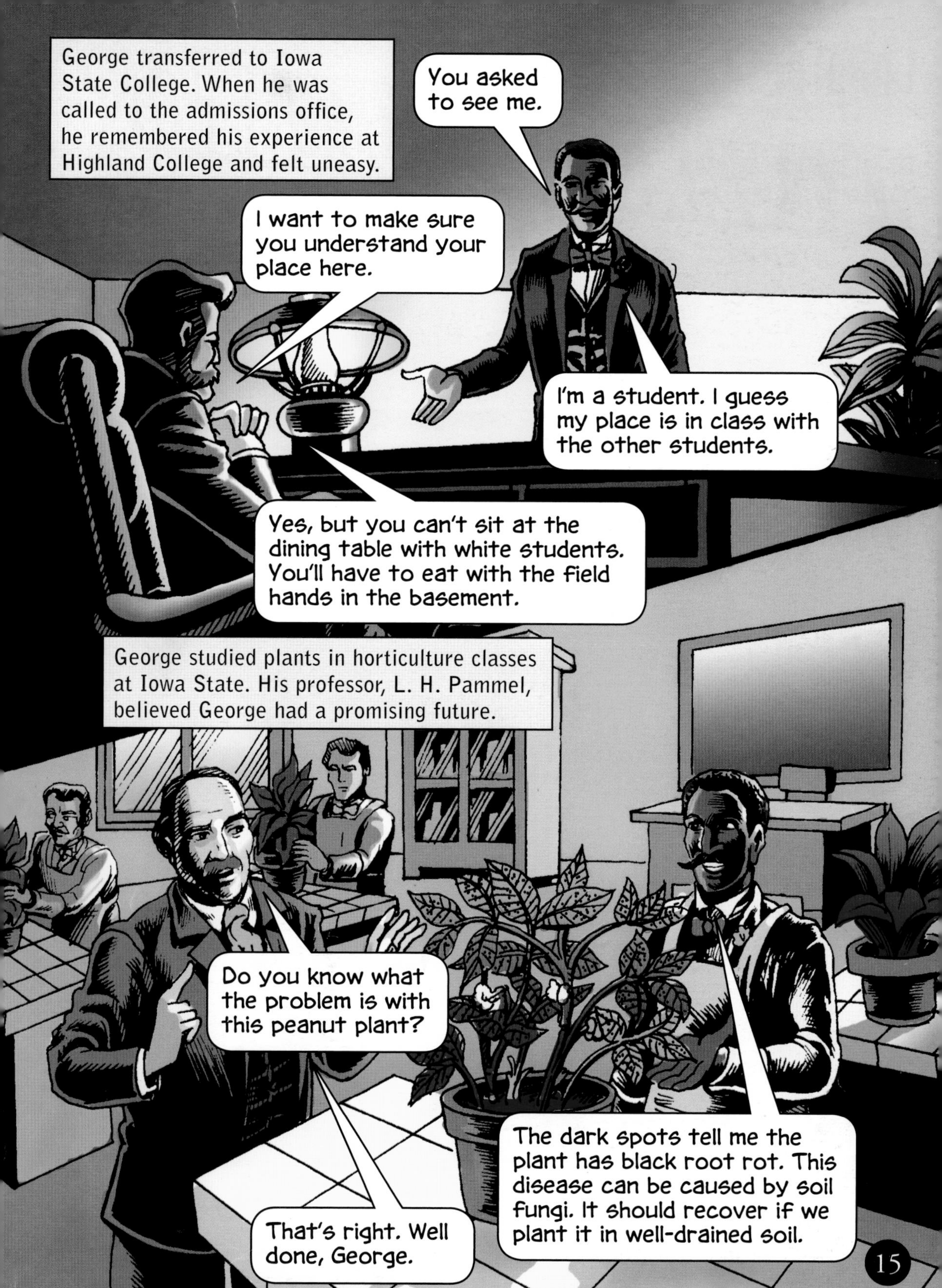
George transferred to Iowa State College. When he was called to the admissions office, he remembered his experience at Highland College and felt uneasy.
You asked to see me.
I want to make sure you understand your place here.
I'm a student. I guess my place is in class with the other students.
Yes, but you can't sit at the dining table with white students. You'll have to eat with the field hands in the basement.
George studied plants in horticulture classes at Iowa State. His professor, L. H. Pammel, believed George had a promising future.
Do you know what the problem is with this peanut plant?
The dark spots tell me the plant has black root rot. This disease can be caused by soil fungi. It should recover if we plant it in well-drained soil.
That's right. Well done, George.

Chapter 3

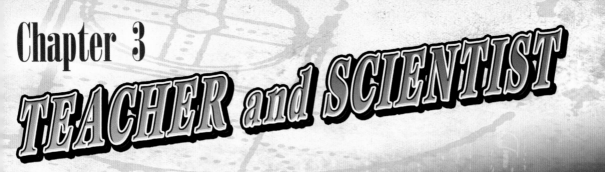

TEACHER and SCIENTIST

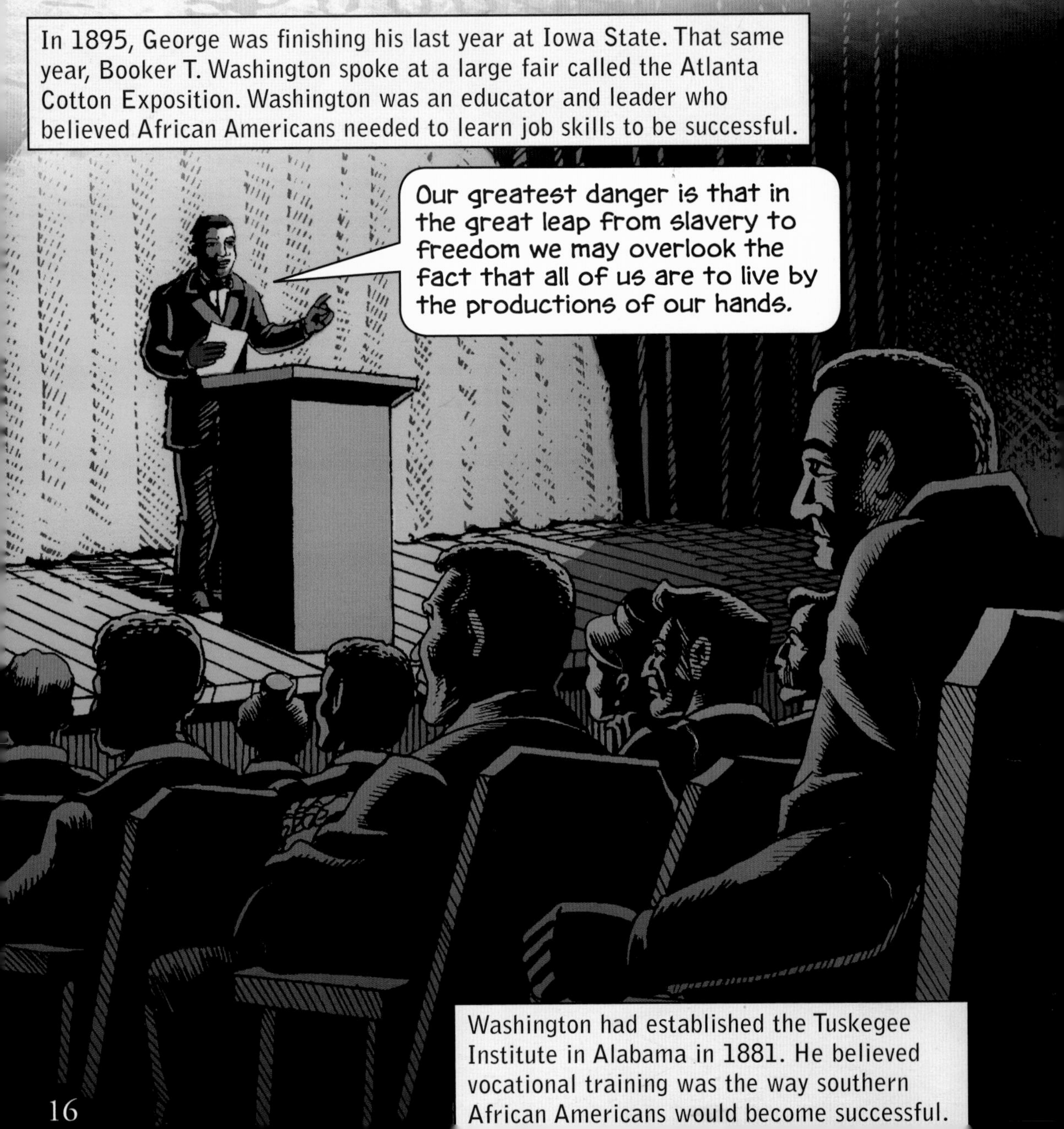
In 1895, George was finishing his last year at Iowa State. That same year, Booker T. Washington spoke at a large fair called the Atlanta Cotton Exposition. Washington was an educator and leader who believed African Americans needed to learn job skills to be successful.
Our greatest danger is that in the great leap from slavery to freedom we may overlook the fact that all of us are to live by the productions of our hands.
Washington had established the Tuskegee Institute in Alabama in 1881. He believed vocational training was the way southern African Americans would become successful.

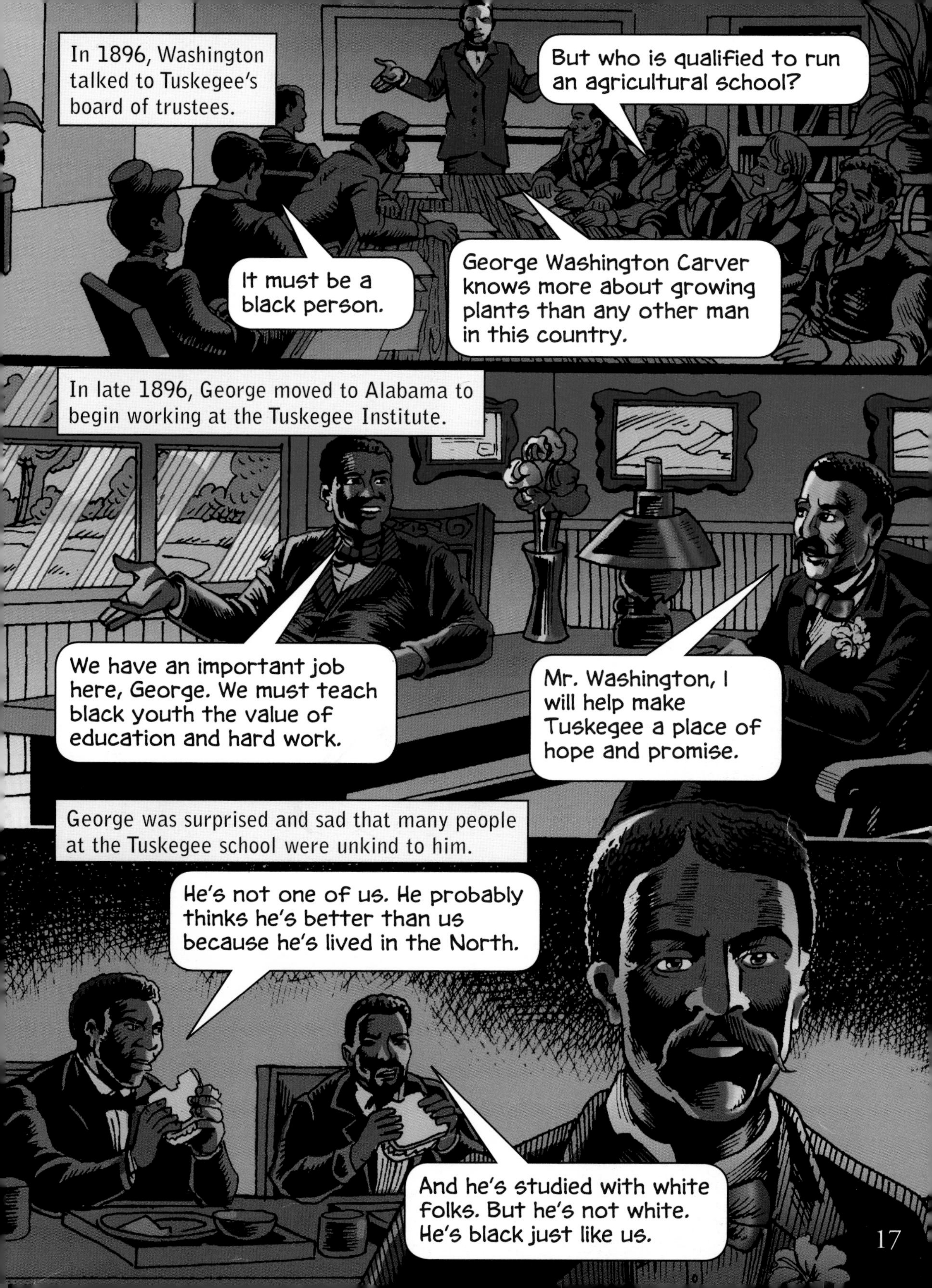
In 1896, Washington talked to Tuskegee's board of trustees.
But who is qualified to run an agricultural school?
It must be a black person.
George Washington Carver knows more about growing plants than any other man in this country.
In late 1896, George moved to Alabama to begin working at the Tuskegee Institute.
We have an important job here, George. We must teach black youth the value of education and hard work.
Mr. Washington, I will help make Tuskegee a place of hope and promise.
George was surprised and sad that many people at the Tuskegee school were unkind to him.
He's not one of us. He probably thinks he's better than us because he's lived in the North.
And he's studied with white folks. But he's not white. He's black just like us.

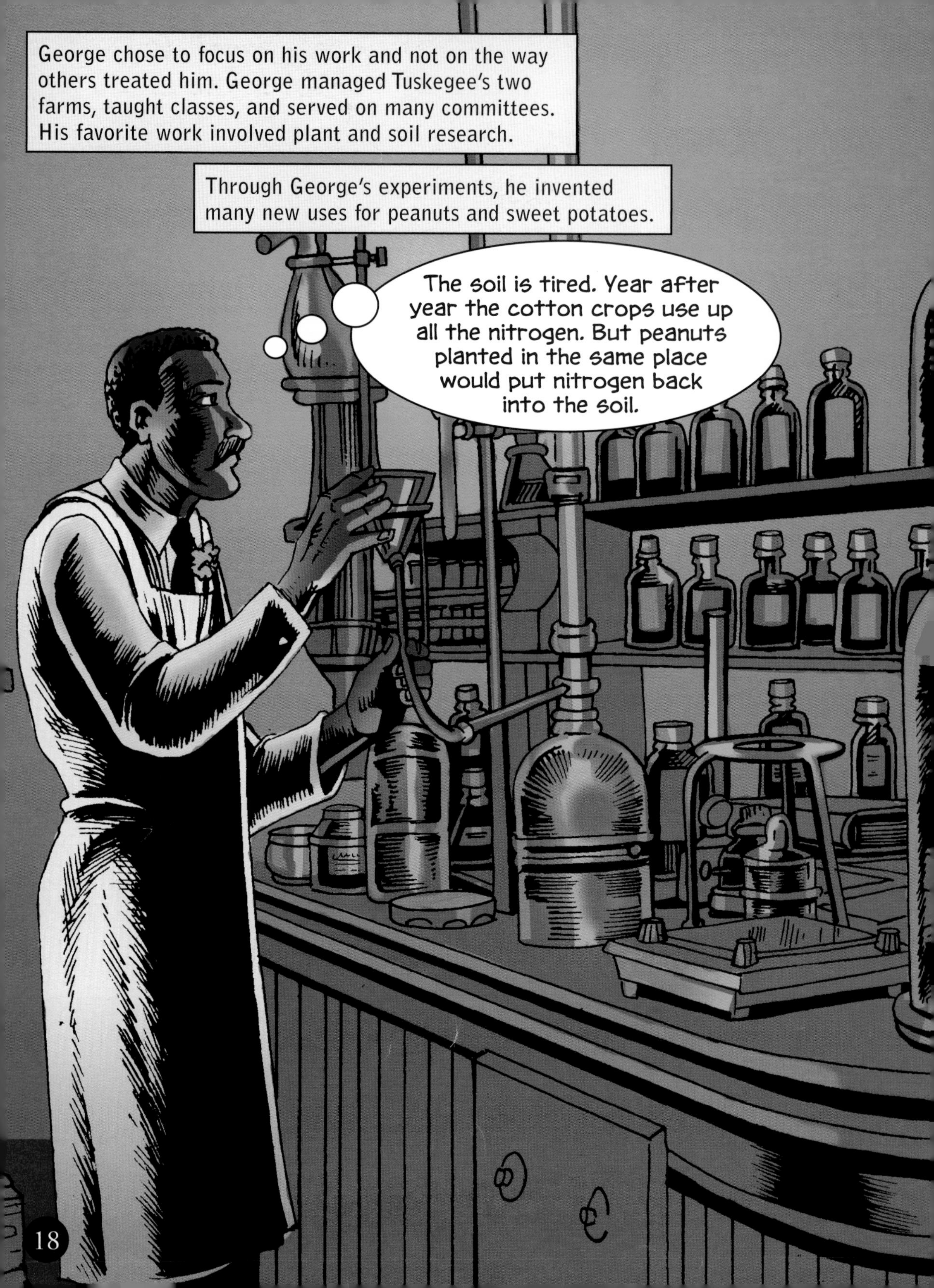
George chose to focus on his work and not on the way others treated him. George managed Tuskegee's two farms, taught classes, and served on many committees. His favorite work involved plant and soil research.
Through George's experiments, he invented many new uses for peanuts and sweet potatoes.
The soil is tired. Year after year the cotton crops use up all the nitrogen. But peanuts planted in the same place would put nitrogen back into the soil.

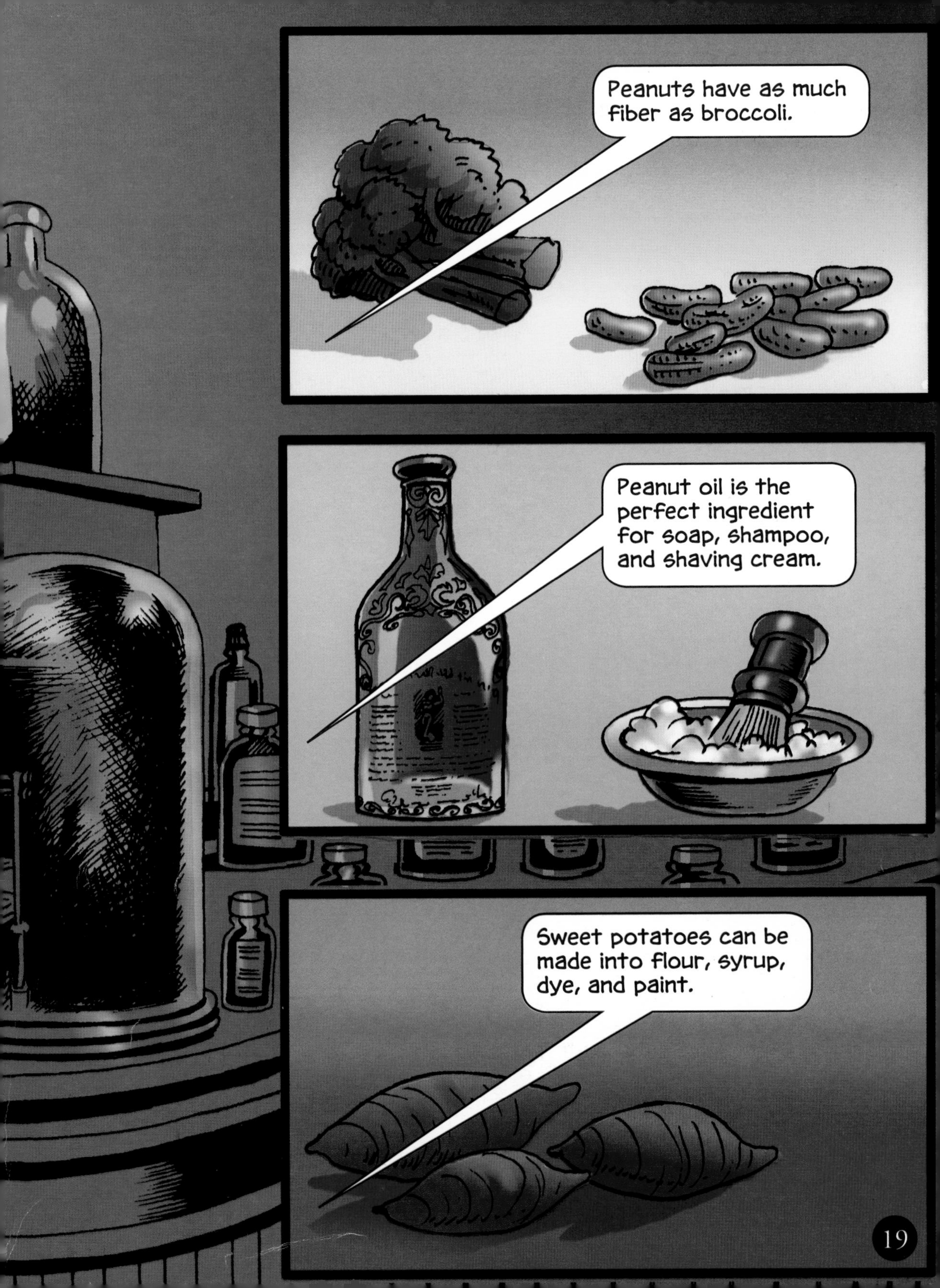

Peanuts have as much fiber as broccoli.
Peanut oil is the perfect ingredient for soap, shampoo, and shaving cream.
Sweet potatoes can be made into flour, syrup, dye, and paint.

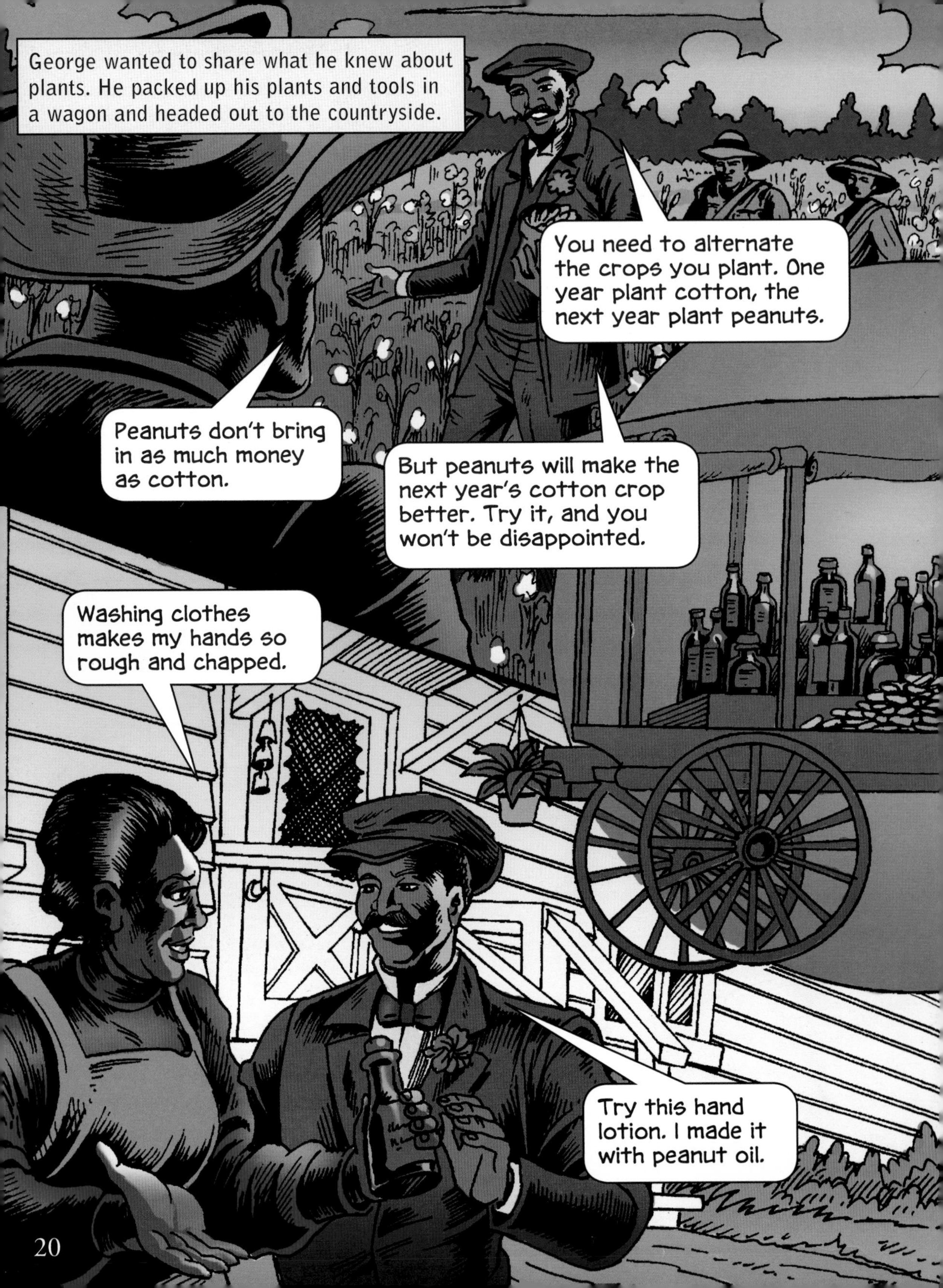
George wanted to share what he knew about plants. He packed up his plants and tools in a wagon and headed out to the countryside.
You need to alternate the crops you plant. One year plant cotton, the next year plant peanuts.
Peanuts don't bring in as much money as cotton.
But peanuts will make the next year's cotton crop better. Try it, and you won't be disappointed.
Washing clothes makes my hands so rough and chapped.
Try this hand lotion. I made it with peanut oil.

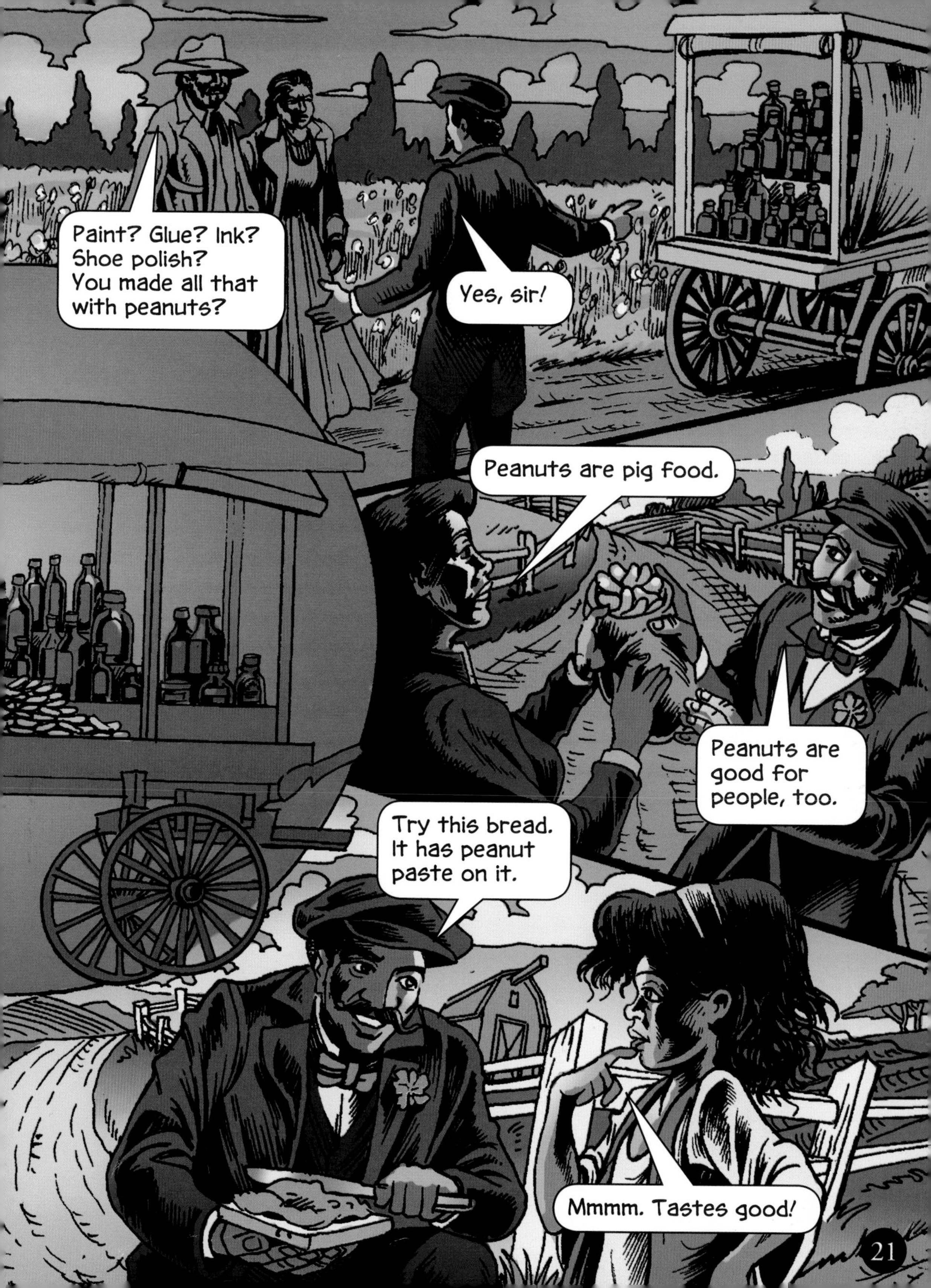
Paint? Glue? Ink?
Shoe polish?
You made all that
with peanuts?
Yes, sir!
Peanuts are pig food.
Peanuts are
good for
people, too.
Try this bread.
It has peanut
paste on it.
Mmmm. Tastes good!

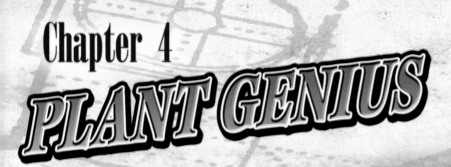

Chapter 4
PLANT GENIUS

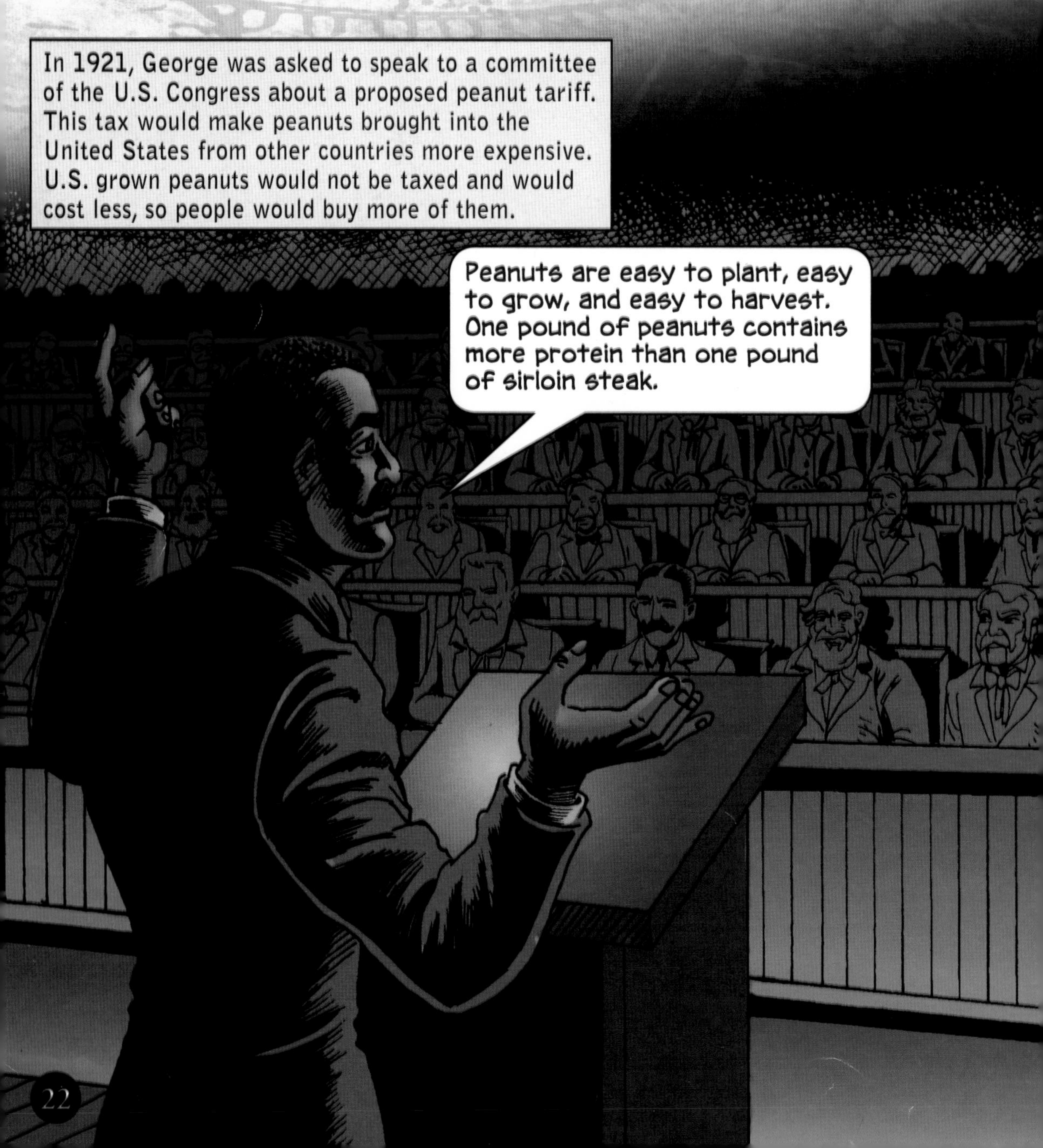
In 1921, George was asked to speak to a committee of the U.S. Congress about a proposed peanut tariff. This tax would make peanuts brought into the United States from other countries more expensive. U.S. grown peanuts would not be taxed and would cost less, so people would buy more of them.
Peanuts are easy to plant, easy to grow, and easy to harvest. One pound of peanuts contains more protein than one pound of sirloin steak.

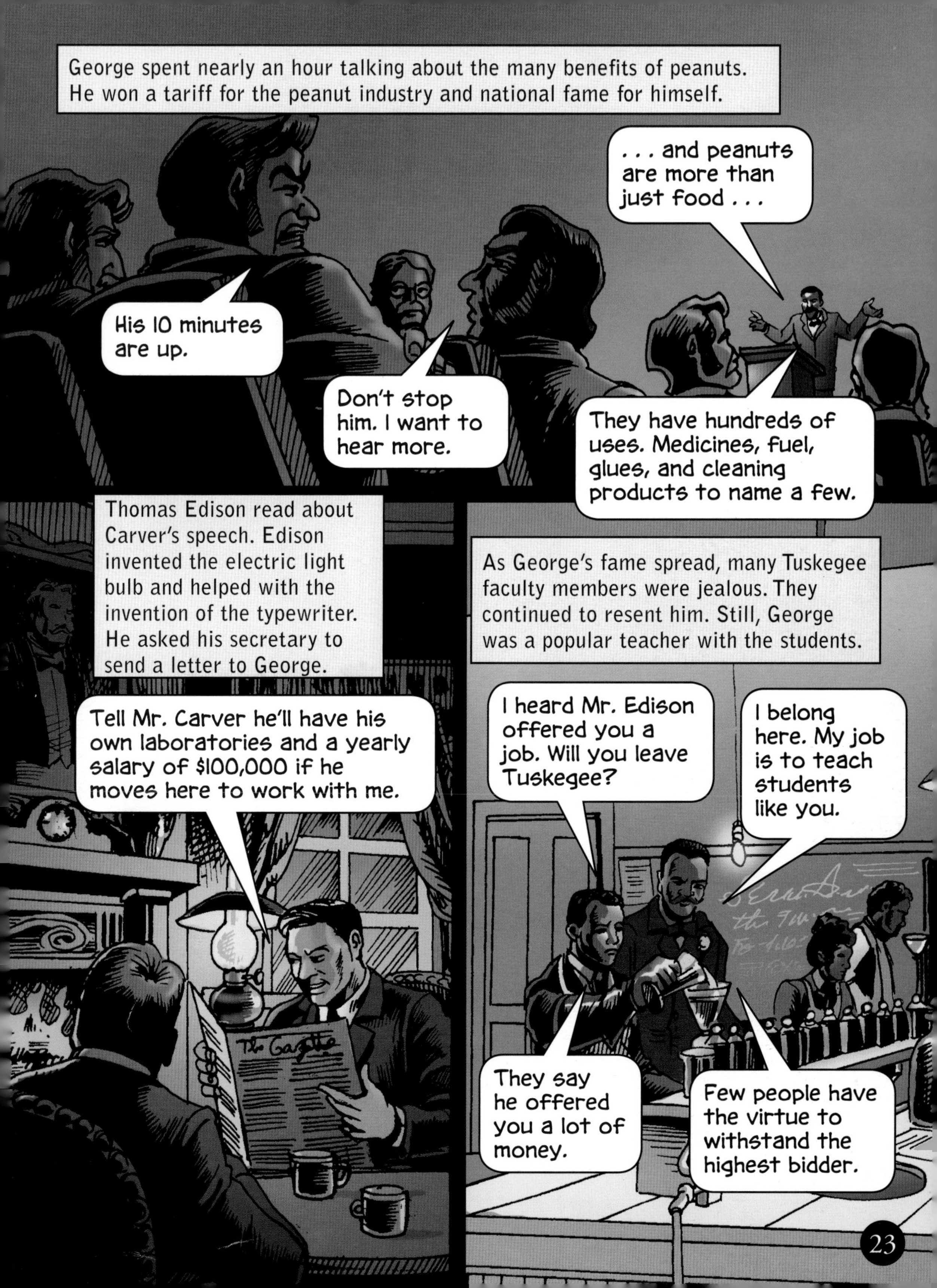
George spent nearly an hour talking about the many benefits of peanuts. He won a tariff for the peanut industry and national fame for himself.
. . . and peanuts are more than just food . . .
His 10 minutes are up.
Don't stop him. I want to hear more.
They have hundreds of uses. Medicines, fuel, glues, and cleaning products to name a few.
Thomas Edison read about Carver's speech. Edison invented the electric light bulb and helped with the invention of the typewriter. He asked his secretary to send a letter to George.
Tell Mr. Carver he'll have his own laboratories and a yearly salary of $100,000 if he moves here to work with me.
The Gazette
As George's fame spread, many Tuskegee faculty members were jealous. They continued to resent him. Still, George was a popular teacher with the students.
I heard Mr. Edison offered you a job. Will you leave Tuskegee?
I belong here. My job is to teach students like you.
They say he offered you a lot of money.
Few people have the virtue to withstand the highest bidder.

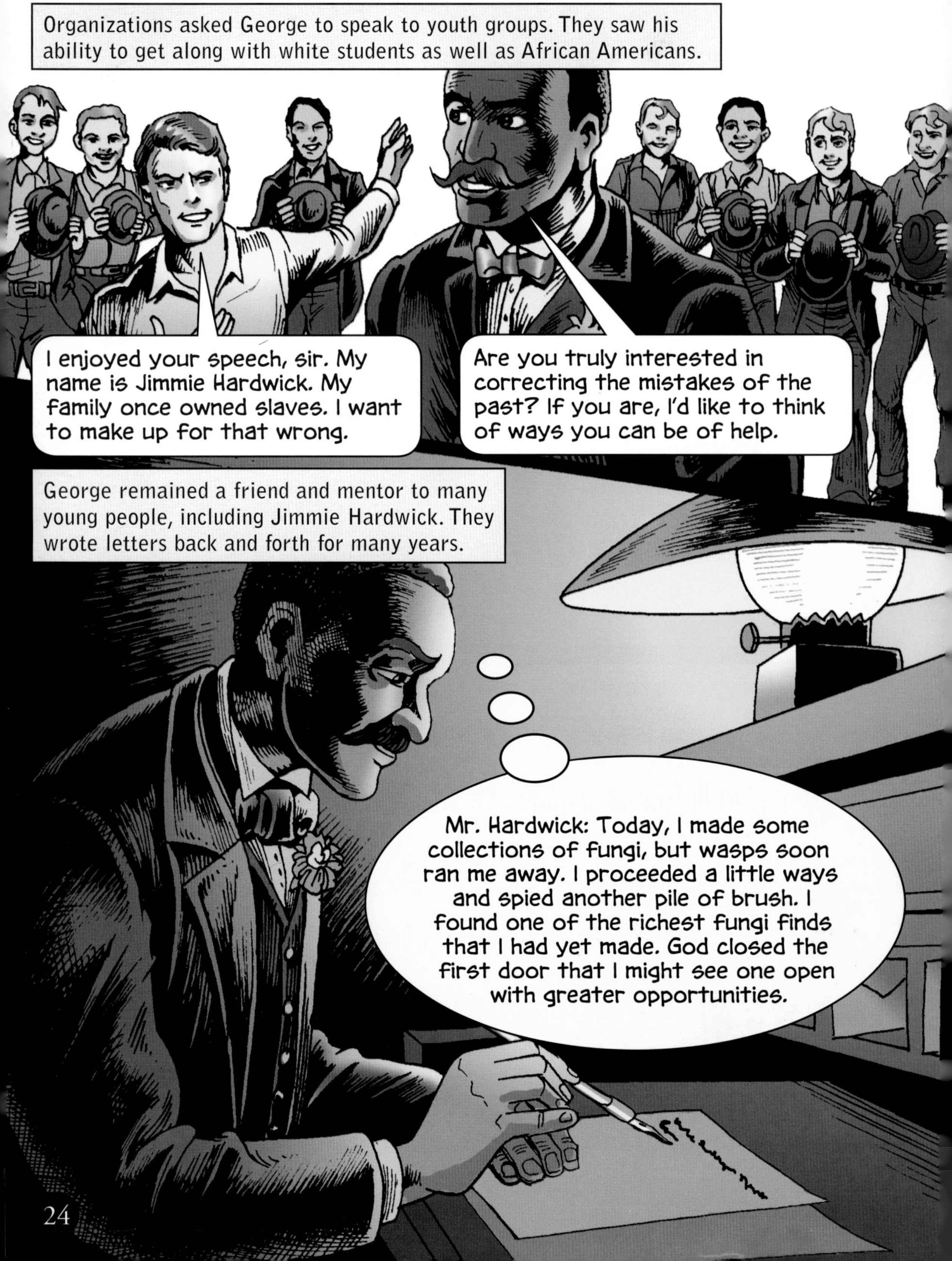
Organizations asked George to speak to youth groups. They saw his ability to get along with white students as well as African Americans.
I enjoyed your speech, sir. My name is Jimmie Hardwick. My family once owned slaves. I want to make up for that wrong.
Are you truly interested in correcting the mistakes of the past? If you are, I'd like to think of ways you can be of help.
George remained a friend and mentor to many young people, including Jimmie Hardwick. They wrote letters back and forth for many years.
Mr. Hardwick: Today, I made some collections of fungi, but wasps soon ran me away. I proceeded a little ways and spied another pile of brush. I found one of the richest fungi finds that I had yet made. God closed the first door that I might see one open with greater opportunities.

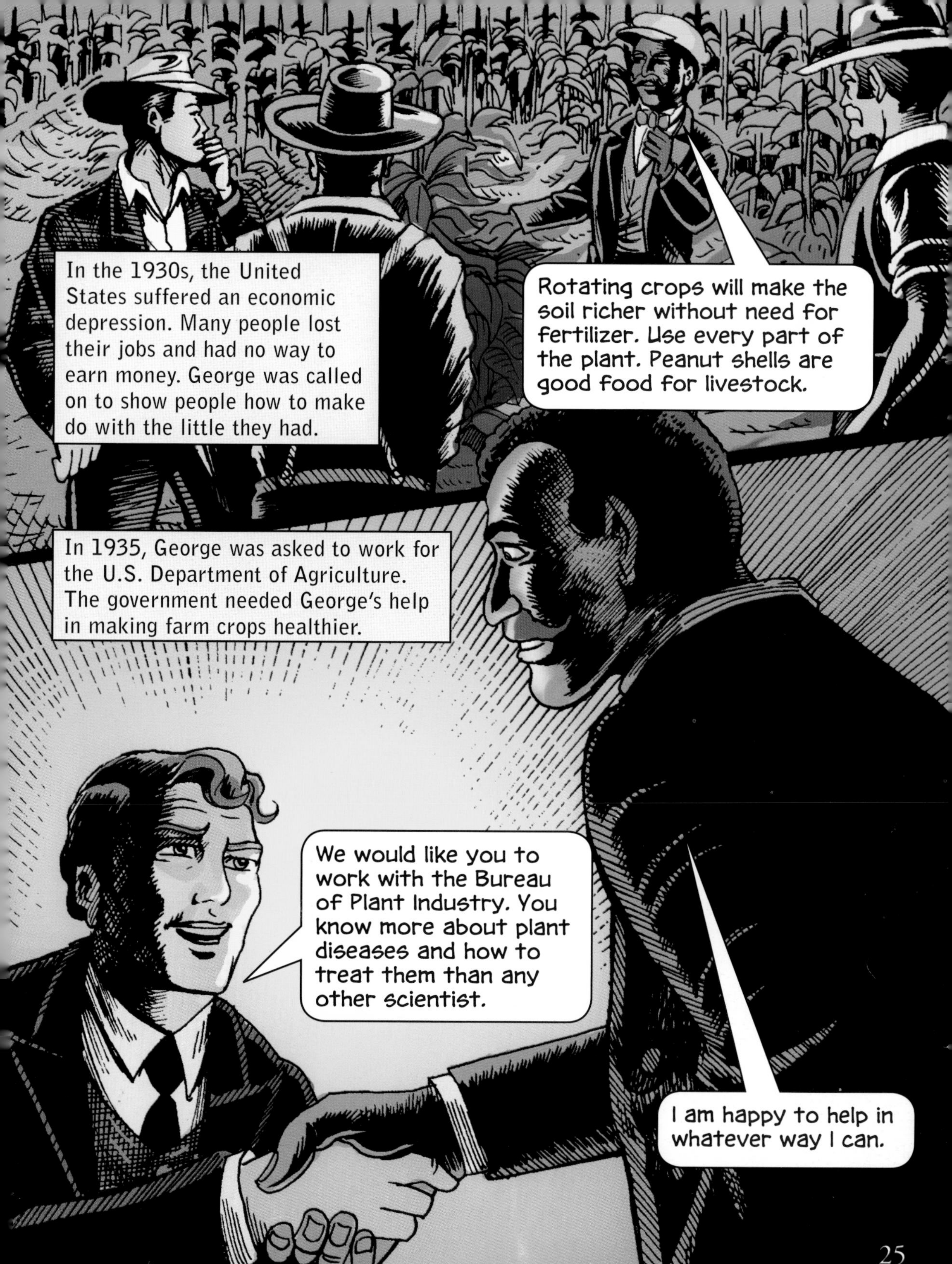
In the 1930s, the United States suffered an economic depression. Many people lost their jobs and had no way to earn money. George was called on to show people how to make do with the little they had.
Rotating crops will make the soil richer without need for fertilizer. Use every part of the plant. Peanut shells are good food for livestock.
In 1935, George was asked to work for the U.S. Department of Agriculture. The government needed George's help in making farm crops healthier.
We would like you to work with the Bureau of Plant Industry. You know more about plant diseases and how to treat them than any other scientist.
I am happy to help in whatever way I can.

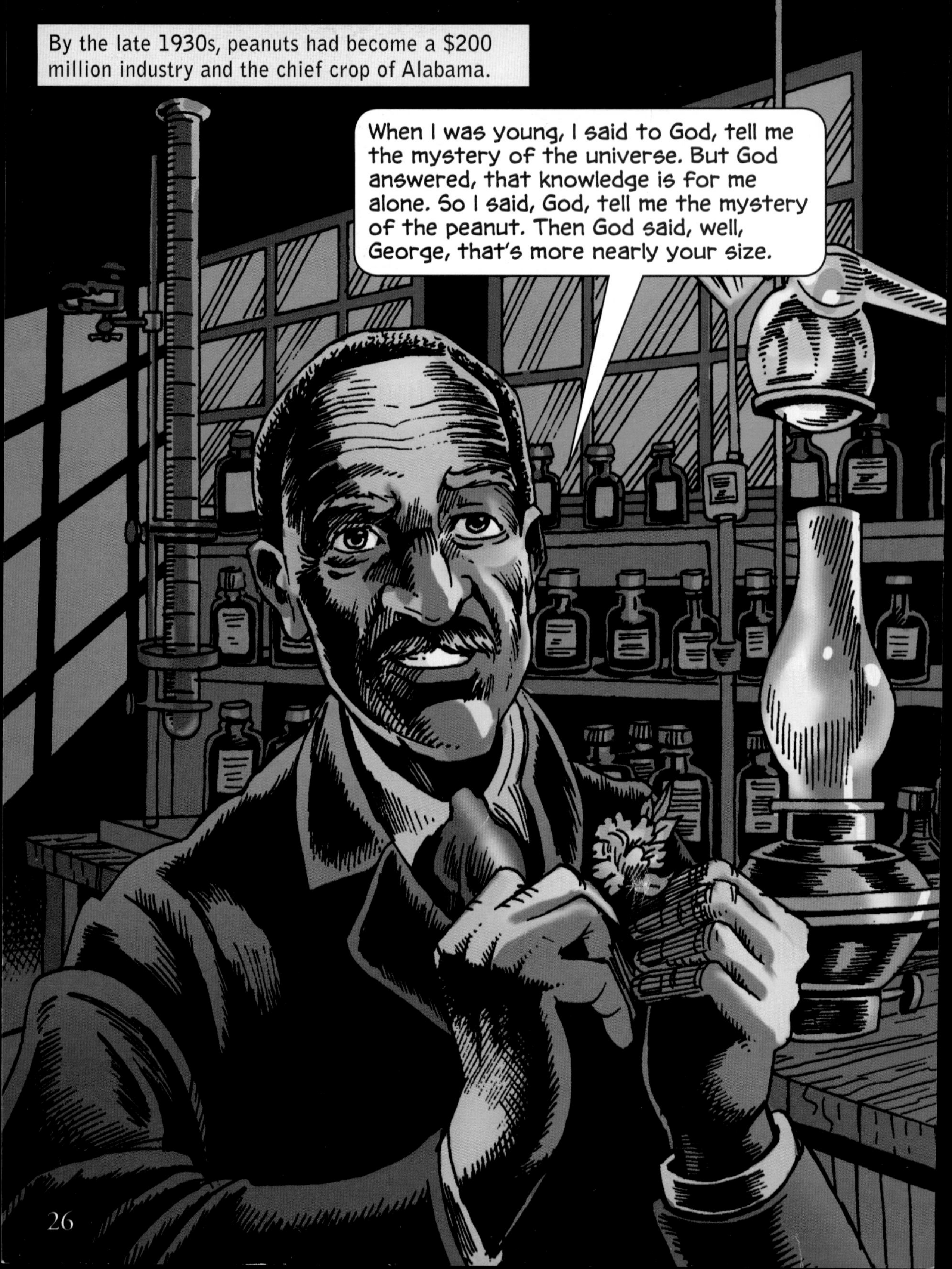
By the late 1930s, peanuts had become a $200 million industry and the chief crop of Alabama.
When I was young, I said to God, tell me the mystery of the universe. But God answered, that knowledge is for me alone. So I said, God, tell me the mystery of the peanut. Then God said, well, George, that's more nearly your size.

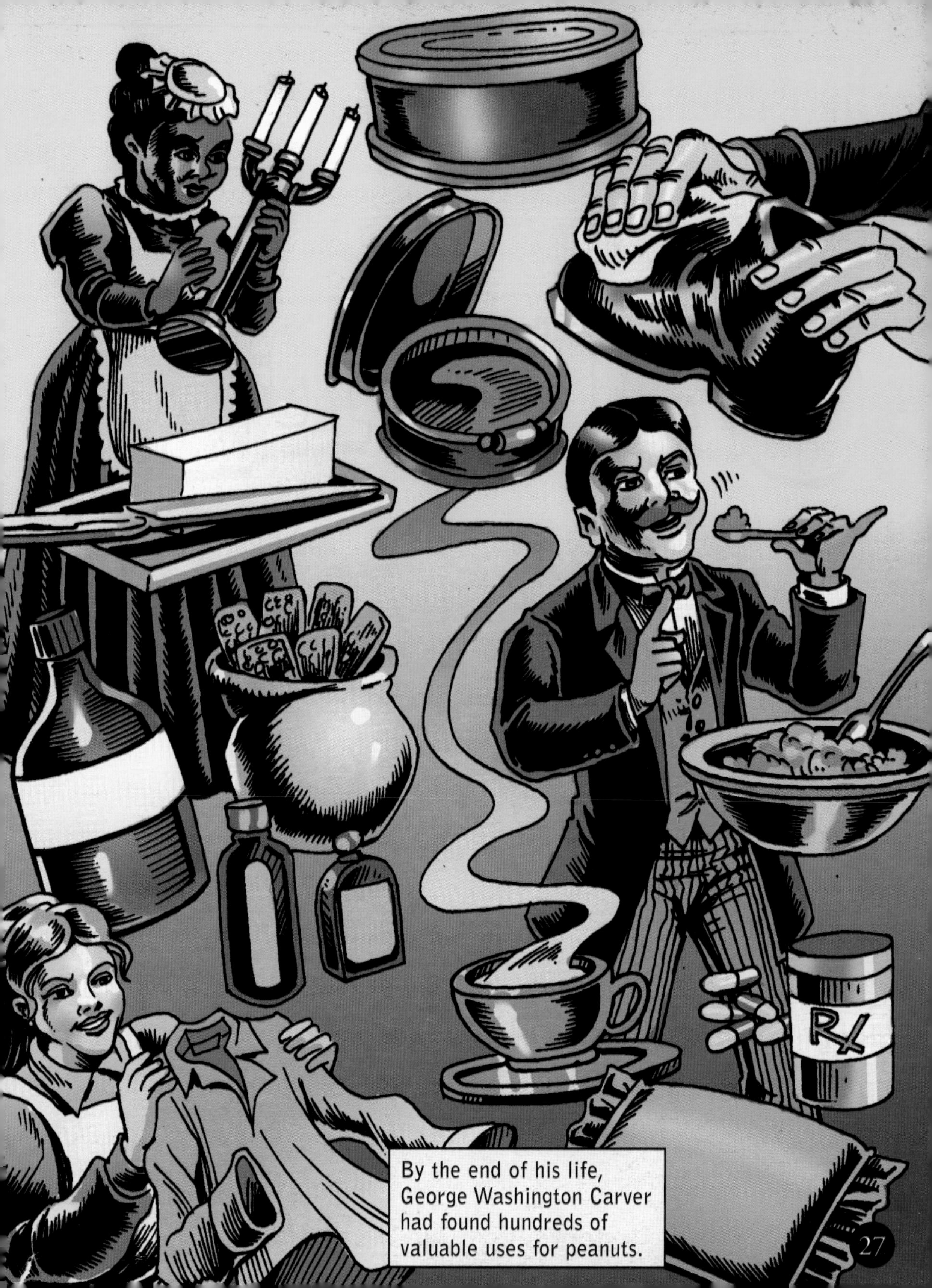
By the end of his life, George Washington Carver had found hundreds of valuable uses for peanuts.

More about

GEORGE WASHINGTON CARVER

- George Washington Carver was born in January 1864, in Diamond Grove, Missouri. He died on January 5, 1943, in Tuskegee, Alabama.

- While in Minneapolis, Kansas, letters George expected from friends and family never arrived for him. He soon discovered another George Carver in the city received his mail in error. George decided to use "W" as his middle initial to end the confusion. People often asked him if the "W" stood for Washington. He decided that it did. From then on he called himself George Washington Carver.

- George Washington Carver held three patents for using peanut oil to make cosmetics and paint. He never profited from his hundreds of discoveries of peanut and sweet potato uses. In 1938, he donated his life savings of more than $30,000 to the George Washington Carver Foundation. The foundation supports science education programs and research in the natural sciences.

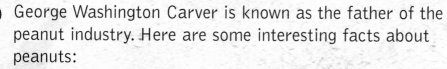 George Washington Carver received many awards and honors. The National Association for the Advancement of Colored People (NAACP) awarded him the Springarn Medal in 1923. Simpson College, where Carver first began his college education, awarded him an honorary Doctor of Science degree in 1928. He received the Theodore Roosevelt Medal in 1939 for distinguished achievement in science.

George Washington Carver is known as the father of the peanut industry. Here are some interesting facts about peanuts:

- Peanuts make up two-thirds of all snack nuts eaten in the United States.
- Peanut butter is the most popular use for peanuts in the United States. Nearly 90 percent of U.S. households eat peanut butter.
- It takes about 540 peanuts to make one 12-ounce jar of peanut butter. There are enough peanuts in one acre to make 3,000 peanut butter sandwiches.

GLOSSARY

abolish (uh-BOL-ish)—to put an end to something officially

bushwacker (BUSH-wak-uhr)—before and during the Civil War, a person who stole slaves and sold them to new owners

fertilizer (FUR-tuh-liz-ur)—a substance added to soil to make crops grow better

fungi (FUHN-jye)—plants that have no leaves, flowers, or roots; mushrooms and molds are both fungi.

horticulture (HOR-tuh-kuhl-chur)—the growing of fruits, vegetables, and flowers

tariff (TA-rif)—a tax charged on goods that are imported or exported

INTERNET SITES

FactHound offers a safe, fun way to find Internet sites related to this book. All of the sites on FactHound have been researched by our staff.

Here's how:

1. *Visit www.facthound.com*
2. Type in this special code **0736854843** for age-appropriate sites. Or enter a search word related to this book for a more general search.
3. Click on the **Fetch It** button.

FactHound will fetch the best sites for you!

READ MORE

Driscoll, Laura. *George Washington Carver: The Peanut Wizard.* Smart About Scientists. New York: Grosset & Dunlap, 2003.

Halvorsen, Lisa. *George Washington Carver: Innovator in Agriculture.* Giants of Science. San Diego, Calif.: Blackbirch Press, 2002.

McKissack, Pat, and Fredrick McKissack. *George Washington Carver: The Peanut Scientist.* Great African Americans. Berkeley Heights, N.J.: Enslow, 2002.

BIBLIOGRAPHY

Edwards, Linda McMurray. *George Washington Carver: Scientist and Symbol.* New York: Oxford University Press, 1981.

Elliott, Lawrence. *George Washington Carver: The Man Who Overcame.* Englewood Cliffs, N.J.: Prentice-Hall, 1966.

Graham, Shirley, and George D. Lipscomb. *Dr. George Washington Carver, Scientist.* New York: J. Messner Inc., 1944.

Holt, Rackham. *George Washington Carver, an American Biography.* Garden City, N.Y.: Doubleday, 1963.

Kremer, Gary R., ed. *George Washington Carver in His Own Words.* Columbia, Missouri: University of Missouri Press, 1987.

INDEX